The Unexploded
Ordnance Bin

Rebecca Foust

SWAN SCYTHE PRESS

ISBN 978-1-930454-47-7

Swan Scythe Press
1468 Mallard Way
Sunnyvale, CA 94087
www.swanscythepress.com

Editor: Robert S. Pesich
Founding Editor: Sandra McPherson
Book Design: Mark Deamer

Printed by The Printer
2810 Cowell Blvd., Davis, California 95618
the-printer.net

Cover Art and Design by Lorna Stevens

Swan Scythe Press books are distributed by
Small Press Distribution, www. spdbooks.org.

Printed in the United States of America.

The Unexploded
Ordnance Bin

Also by Rebecca Foust

Paradise Drive (Press 53, 2015)

God, Seed: Poetry & Art about the Natural World,
with Lorna Stevens (Tebot Bach, 2010)

All That Gorgeous, Pitiless Song (Many Mountains
Moving Press, 2010)

Mom's Canoe (Texas Review Press, 2009)

Dark Card (Texas Review Press, 2008)

Contents

II

III

Acknowledgements

These poems were first published, sometimes in a variant form, as follows:

Academy of American Poets, Poem-A-Day: "Third Gratitude," originally under the title "Abeyance"

American Literary Review: "Little Brown Bat"

Bellingham Review: "Sufferance"

Birmingham Poetry Review: "the unexploded ordnance bin"

Concho River Review: "Vehicular"

The Cortland Review: "valentine"

Crab Creek Review: "Autism"

Fire on Her Tongue (Two Sylvias Press 2011): "Flame"

The Hudson Review: "Like Birders" and "Only"

The Humanist: "after the dream act"

Journal of the American Medical Association: "Compound. Depressed. Fracture." and "Head Injury Odyssey"

Mudlark: "spec house foundation cut into ridge"

Narrative: "Perseids"

North American Review: "Iconostasis," winner of 2015 James Hearst Prize (Jane Hirshfield) and "First Gratitude," originally under the title "Gratitude," Second Place for the 2014 James Hearst Prize (Martin Espada)

Pleiades: "Failed Aubade"

Poet Lore: "Miguel"

Poetry East: "Echo"

Prairie Schooner: "Everything Golden Is Spilled"

Seattle Review: "Blame"

South Carolina Review: "rapture/rupture"

Southern Indiana Review: "The Deer"

Valparaiso Poetry Review: "Prodigal"

Van Gogh's Ear: "dolphin"

Western Humanities Review: "Moon"

Zyzzyva: "Remembrance of Things Past" and "Requiem Mass for the Yuma 14"

"Third Gratitude," was reprinted in *How Lovely the Ruins* (Spiegel & Grau 2017), in *Zoom In… Individual and Society* (Schöningh Verlag 2017), and the *Huffington Post*, 11/19/16, "18 Compassionate Poems to Help You Weather Uncertain Times."

The ticking is the bomb. —Nick Flynn

Only

O love, this happened or it did not.
In a room with green walls

my son was born. The cord was torn
too soon, so they cut off

his head to save his heart. He
lived for a long time.

For a long time there was no breath or cry.
When finally he spoke,

he spoke the wide, whorled leaves of corn.
He spoke the crickets

in clusters beneath the sheaves, he sang
the soil in. He sang the wind

in the dune and hush of ebb tide. Some say
he died. Some say he died.

I

Autism

Brave new mother, she refused to cast salt
over her left shoulder
and guided her son's first steps under ladders,
laughing at their broken selves
in the shards of a dropped mirror.
Then, science and myth
were fictions they could ignore.

Now she opens the door to his room
to consider his things:
frayed parts of a motherboard,
a chipped prism. A cast-iron lock rusted shut,
a Botts' dot burnished
like scrimshaw. Flint flakes, negative space
of an arrowhead's edge.

In a less amber time still illiterate
in entrails, stirred ash, and bones
of small birds, she'd have tipped it all
into the trash. But she's seen these things aligned
to make a jeweled matrix, heard them
sung to under the modem's hum.
A mother, like any seer,
walks the dark corridor of future alone,
and fear is the lamp and the book
that teaches respect for the family totem.

Perseids

When the real star died and fell, I knew the others for tricks,
trompe l'oeil on insides of eyelids. But it was no trick
when that star larger than sky fell out of my sky,

shock of arc-then-black. My son has chest pains again.
I thought we were past this. When he was a child,
it was easy to hold his hand all night so he wouldn't die—

trace toxins in cereal, the new mole on his left little toe
—I sang him back to sleep and the next day
 he was off again, climbing branches I couldn't reach

or hunching all day over a fixed lens, knotting a fish line
fine as an eyelash. He collects horseshoe-crab trash,
knowing and naming each slender spire;

once I broke one and hid the pieces, but he missed it later,
back to croon to his darlings, constellated in precise
patterns in the sky of his bedroom floor.

He's tall now, with a beard. The astral map is in pieces,
just as real stars come unmoored and fall
into flaming comets. Power fails,

EKGs skip and stutter, MRIs hum, then blink off. Boys
he knew in school come home from Iraq without
legs. He trolls the internet for side effects

of medicine taken to decrease the world's discomfort
with him. "Rarely fatal" *doesn't mean never,*
and what logic doesn't whet each day's edge

with fear? *I could die, I might die, we all die. I'll die.*
Maybe tonight, alone in his sleep. *Don't get mad,
Mom.* We've done all the tests twice,

but being alive means proving a negative. So how
can we go on believing each day won't be the one
that flames out? When he walks in his sleep,

his eyes are open and dark night-terror pools. *Shh,* now
he's dropping off, worry lines etching his forehead,
shape of his mouth sucked into the neck

of his T-shirt. Overhead, stars arc across the dark sky
making small curved rips, and the light leaks out.

the unexploded ordnance bin

our son found the hollow shell
snub-nosed & finned
& looking like an Acme cartoon bomb
where we raked for clams
he wanted to keep it
& we wanted to let him

even the old oysterman wanted
to let him   but we'd read about
the shell found & kept
for three weeks by a boy
in Oregon before the powder
dried   & it went off

we took a few minutes
to snap photos of our son,
an ordinary boy then,
putting the shell under his sister's pillow
& pretending to launch it
at all the foods that made him gag

at the police station
the desk sergeant crooked
a thumb towards the dune
with its big metal bin & warning sign
once a month   he said   we set them off
& it really lights the place up

it's too small to be seen
the gene causing autism   but I imagine it
anyway with snub nose & fins
& powder waiting to dry   first words
blown off & away like the fingers
of that Oregon boy

whose mom's grief I used to feel safe from
who let her son keep his bomb
in ignorance or faith strong as
my own caution that led in the end
to the same spectacular
dismemberment of the future

& I wonder what it would look like
the bin for safe disposal of genes
that can ruin children
& I think maybe it's my own body
or rather   the body
without children or rather the body

that's lucky   or belonging
to someone still living
in ignorance & improbable faith
or maybe   the bin
is the world when to be human
was all promise & radiance

unwinding dawn mudflats
into long   wide shining ribbons
pink as a new baby's gums
& elsewhere a family
in a warm illuminated room
is eating steamed clams

or just any ordinary dinner
as if it weren't going to blow all to hell
any second   all those bright dreams
lit up like tracer fire
over the dark dunes   like the Perseids
only not at all   like the Perseids

Everything Golden Is Spilled

You were born and your hour was silver,
new moonlight strewn

on dark ground. Pearls, seeds, wide banks
of clouds, your bright hair,

your damp, sleeping lap-weight, scalp's
yolky chuff, tug at the nipple,

the universe contracted to suck and glow;
grain, drops of rain,

dreams for a time ripening and bending
wheat weighted with seed.

When did the season turn? Now drained
down, gone—we are

still in it, but the world has grown old,
and I want that bud

of boy back, packed with what might
yet bloom, each spiraled sepal

still sealed, and nothing, nothing revealed.

rapture/rupture

watching the wheel chair make
its long slow arc   the child's face slack
with what could be read

as rapture   a mother might well
thank God for the intact body of her own son
& also for the tiny stars of wood violets

the sun's rays shot through a cloud
a finch's sentence scribbled over & over
the wide expanse of a fallow field

needle in a haystack times ten
the chance my son would get this gene
my hand the only hand

he's held in two decades
a bitterness   yes   but I'm grateful for fire
and years   & the uses of gauze

for sparing your eyes   & my eyes
from your eyes   & that a wound   when
it's cauterized   seeps less

spec house foundation cut into ridge

often in the dawn or dusk
and one night by moonlight

I saw them there
picking a delicate way

down the bank
on a hidden path   ripple

of silver on leaves
& out steps a fawn

shy as my fey boy
all long limbs   dark eyes

and twitch
of ear in the still canyon air

they lived there once   a family
of deer   they lived there

The Deer

It came mid-sentence, the blow so nearly not a blow, the light
shattered and flung into fog, scattered shards
blooming chrysanthemum then dissolving away,
a Roman candle illuming the night

then fading a great mute sigh of O. The night stumbled,
the blow repeated and muffled below, the way
a stopped sneeze staggers the body—light eclipsed,
scatter of force imploded—

cantata of grace notes sunk in a chord. We ask God's grace
in these moments, fearing the night, how
a balked reflex can slug the heart and block the breath.
This is the blow that matters. This is the way

the car goes on, out of the light. This is the deer conjured
in retrograde grace, the ardent arc of her body
scoring the night and trailing bright streamers
of glass and mist. The blow felt, at first,

like a glancing blow. So much light at that moment,
astral scatter blazing the windshield. Just a graze
and she'd rise and bound away. Except she did
not, and we foundered while night

reclaimed our lane, what-was-below caught, then cleared.
Had there been a blow? We knew the way without
our right headlight; home, and the garden hose,
its scatter of water across the hood,

then rain's final grace. This is the way it happens.
You are crossing a road at night. A blow,
a scatter of light that you yourself make.
Grace, if it's quick or in rain. The car will go on.

Vehicular

You were sure it was only a deer, dead
the second we hit it, so we didn't stop
but pressed on for spring break

in Orlando and never spoke of it again,
not once in forty years. It was near dawn
on the Georgia Interstate, you driving

all night in sheeting sleet and rain.
There was a blow, or not, then he was down
—splayed, long-limbed and already past—

it happened so fast I thought I'd dreamt
the pale vertical slice of his face
between ice-clabbered wipers, the shudder

under the tires, first front, then back.
But I was wrong. The dreaming came later.

Blame

after the record in <u>People v. Vandross</u>

the olive tree that dropped its great gout
of dark fruit onto asphalt, for the swerve
and spinout etched in fresh virgin press;
blame the natural law that made helpless
bodies attract and collide then come to rest
in the acacia-treed canyon. The driver sat
behind the wheel, side not pierced—not yet.
Yes he was drunk, but only with joy
for the lovely lithe boy now fused with the car,
shrink-wrapped in leather and steel
and veiled by the webbed windshield; the boy
who sang backup gospel like a bruised angel
and was the hope of his whole Bronx block.
Blame the last bright note that opened his throat
and sank into pollen and dust.

Compound. Depressed. Fracture.

His home, before the bus ran it down,
was a cardboard box.
A piece of his skull was trepanned
and housed
in a hollow that lay near his heart.

Humpty Dumpty was put back
together again, and you took
your son home. But when you let go
the sitter (no rehab would take him
so long as he needed a sitter),

he fell again. Such interrupture.
How can a mother tend to her orchard?
The sun continues its consort with bones
and seeds, skin no more
than a wet petal translucent on pavement.

Your eyes bell with water, salt is poured
on the roots of your heart.
Words are strung like beads in the dark
of the crazy ward,
each hour a weal on the body of days

and you are amputated at the four points,
an exiled samovar
that never will work again,
the outermost shell of a Russian doll
tragedy that began with a birth, or before.

Head Injury Odyssey

Prepare as if for an ocean voyage, the doctor said;
gather your loaves of bread and flagons
of wine; make peace with your gods.

But he didn't say they'd be sailing in a balsa-wood
boat, or that their boy would be foundering too,
somewhere ahead in the mist

at the helm of his own fragile skiff, that they'd
separate in storms and boiling straits
not once, twice, but endless times

choosing between equally untenable tacks, or that
he'd be bound to the bedrails, ears sealed
to slip past the sirens singing

promises of no more pain; that he, enchanted to stone
by Calypso, would forget home and have
to sail the last leg blind and alone,

or that memory would be swallowed by whirlpools,
caves, forests of pine, so many cattle
slaughtered, so much wine

poured out on dry ground, or that when he came home
he'd be changed, so much they'd have to look
for any sign to know him by:

his birthmark still there under the great, new scar
and Bill his old dog getting up from his bed
to meet their son at the door.

Like Birders

Shared obsession and fixed gaze, six of them brood
over three rebuilt monitors.

Taken out to dinner, they speak acronym—RPG, DM,
LCD—the way you might parse

beak sizes and shapes, flight patterns, and the mottling
on the breast of the male spotted grouse.

I want to say read a book, get a job, meet a girl, make
anything real happen. They occupy spots

on a grid penciled on butcher paper. Eyes closed, each boy
plots his plan for survival.

Friends drowned in frozen fens, the enemy everywhere hidden,
and burned is the grail and the ark,

but each hand is certain, holding the die; knowing by pitch
or array of note which creature roosts, or lurks in the dark.

First Gratitude

He speaks, and when we speak, he understands.
Not like my friend's boy who tap-taps the board
behind his bed, not using his hands,

who taps the wood with his forehead in a kind
of mandarin code. A light's gone underground:
no speech, but her son can gesture and understand

so he's better off than the steel-cribbed child, blind
even to pain, left at the Home, whose eyes are wide
and blue. Who began by sucking his hands,

then his teeth came in. What's left of his hands
are mittened in gauze and bound to his side.
Our son speaks. He talks, we talk. He understands.

And this is the crux: when he talks, we understand
if he hungers or thirsts, is sad or scared.
He was not left in his crib, we put books in his hands.

He's not wild pinned down in a trap, chained
to his own spine, gnawing the only way out or in.
He speaks. He holds a pen. He understands.
He has all of all of his fingers. On both of his hands.

II

Miguel

His mother cleans my house twice a month
and no, she doesn't have papers.
He is every healthy nine-month-old child
in his limpid perfection and re-invention of grin,
llama-lashed eyes, toffee skin.
He sings out round, hollow vowels: dog sounds,
hello sounds, good-bye sounds.
He blows me a fat-fisted kiss. Sometimes
I'm allowed to hold him or take him outside
into our picket-fenced yard
where I teach him to let the dog sniff his hand.

After the election, I think of my son
who under Hitler might have worn the black badge
of the mentally impaired and been euthanized.
When Miguel visits again, I can't see him
without remembering the photos taken by my father,
an army medic at Dachau. You know those horrors
of boxcars and bodies, smokestacks and smoke.
But widen the lens just a little and you'd see
not far from the camp, the neatly fenced gardens,
thatched roofs, and doors painted blue.

In one photo, an obscene tangle of pale skin
and tattoos, with villagers milling around
dressed as I might dress to run errands:
comfortable, practical, warm. Their tidy homes
were about as close to the camp
as the ICE Deportation Center in the town
next to mine. In another photo, the villagers
dig a mass grave while soldiers stand guard.
My fingers curl around something hard
and unforgiving as I am handed the spade
and made to dig.

Little Brown Bat

1.

That you must fall to fly. That you can live two decades
or more. That you have young like we do, one per year.

That you make a rich milk to feed your pup and to keep it
warm fold it between your wings.

That you eat every day half your weight in mosquitoes, found
by echolocation one winged speck at a time.

That you hibernate in utter torpor, absorbing the fat you've
stored, a very precise amount.

That you were, on that July night, a shy, soft thing, a vibration
just brushing my left eyebrow.

That you, once unnumbered as Dante's autumn leaves, die in
droves from eating the insects

we poison. That you are cut down by wind turbines, not the
blades but the drop in air pressure popping you

like kernels of corn. That you swoop and career arcs traced by
the streetlights of my childhood summers.

That when my father taught me to swat down a bat with a
broom—a brown mouse with wings and soft ear tufts—

then to bring down the hammer, cleared his throat and looked
away. That you rarely are rabid

and never drink blood—you eat fruit and in a day half your
weight in mosquitoes—that you pollinate

our orchards in summer and in winter sleep in caves, upside
down, furled like buds with your young clasped inside.

2.

Magnified, *Geomyces destructans* is branched and fletched
like a blue snowflake,

and it blooms over your face, body and wings, etching your
flesh in terrible symmetry,

and when you most need to be still, it disturbs you, makes you
move in your sleep, burning the fat

you've stored, a very precise amount that assumes a dormant
bat, one who does not stir,

but you do stir in your deep sleep, and starve, and fall. Not to fly
but to make a thick layer

on the cave floor, fur and small bones crunched underfoot by
Cavers who tell the Scientists,

who begin to study and count you, carrying the spores on their
boots from cave to cave.

3.

That you starve in your sleep in such numbers you tuft a carpet
of plush, then bones,

that in trying to save you we only spread the disease. That it
takes twelve months to gestate and wean one pup.

That in a single cave your number fell from a quarter million to
thirty-five bats, last year—

make that thirty-four—less tonight's shy, soft vibration near my
left eyebrow

that, sick and confused, staggered and sank like a small tangled kite into the toilet behind me.

That you were a mother or a father trying to feed your young who trust you will save them by leaving,

or—like those immigrant children—by sending them away, children held and fed just long enough

to complete the paperwork to return them to where we won't have to watch them die, sent away

like autistic children once were sent away, their flapping hands unseen, their strange cries unheard.

That, when afraid, we revert to lessons taught in our childhood; we shrink from the least vibration of air,

we plug our ears and close our eyes against any flailing; we look away from what we've been taught we can't bear,

we avert our gaze, and when we can, we flush it away.

after the dream act is revoked

it's time to get my hair cut again & the dream act
just got rolled back   what can i do
get in the car   keep the appointment
preserve etiquette   the economy   routine
so stupid   stupid   stupid   what can i do
pick fruit for a pie   sweep the floor
feed the dog   call my reps   send emails
knit a hat   go to a march   write this dumb poem
phone my kids who I can reasonably hope
will not get shot going out for milk   or sling-shot
back to a country that vomited them up
in fire & thirst & dismemberment
to land here with no guarantees
but what it says in the constitution   oh   right
that applies only to   "citizens"
& those the law defines as   "persons"
such as some corporations   but not to all human beings
& as per the 3/5 clause and Dred Scott   not even always
to all of each human being   oh   right
that what's-a-person thing is a very vexing question
well then   what about my-country-'tis-of-thee
freedom   fairness & civil rights   a government
governed by the will of its people but   who are its people
what do we mean by "people"   by "its"
I can play this game all day long   the people
I know are mostly decent
if catatonic with abundance & consumption & god
& their screens   & oh god this hair
really needs to be cut   this floor swept
the dog fed   these apples
should be picked before they rot   who does not
abhor waste   what can i do
what can i do   what will it take for us
to see refugees as refugees   not carpetbaggers
but people like our own brothers & sisters & parents & children
so many children who can't swim keep crossing that river
the fires our CIA set still raging behind them

& when will we admit the pogrom is here
& people are people are people are people are
people are   already beginning   to disappear

Remembrance of Things Past

He was nine when he walked a continent
of desert, holding hands

with strangers on Devil's Highway, the same
road the Yuma Fourteen

took when they died. The journey north
began with prayers and tears

beneath an arch twined with plastic flowers
and included a hundred miles

of dust and no water, razor wire, gunshots,
and a boat ride at night

with twenty others packed into a metal hull.
What he recalls:

none knew how to swim. Darkness. Crush.
Cold. Wet. Oil drums

for latrines. An engine that coughed, then
choked on a silence

lap-lapped by waves. A lullaby of cries
and soft curses, the click-click

of beads. Water that was endless and black.
The odor that evokes

his childhood, he says, is no madeleine
but instead a rich stew

of sweat, shit, and vomit. Struck match
and spilled gasoline.

Requiem Mass for the Yuma Fourteen

Beyond the border they could smell the rain.
It smelled like freedom. Freedom and home.
The desert composes its requiem.

The oldest was sixty, his grandson thirteen.
One wore new jeans, one carried a comb.
Beyond the border they could smell the rain.

They got lost, then they lost their water. The sun
was a furnace blast. Dust. Thirst. Delirium,
the desert composing its requiem.

Vampire air. Heat that bakes flesh off bone.
Hands fretworked with spines, mouths crammed
with quartz, they smelled the rain.

The boy dreamt saguaro was bread and the stones
were stars. He heard tall, cool-winged seraphim
rehearsing a *requiem aeternam*.

He made a neat stack of his clothes, and at dawn
he lay down. He burst like a ripe sunset, a plum.
Beyond the border, you can smell the rain.
The desert composes its requiem.

Iconostasis

on the YouTube examination of the body of Hamza Ali
al-Khateeb, 13, tortured and killed by the Syrian government

For the plastic parted and peeled back to reveal him,
a panel woven in linen.

For his hands, a hummingbird's thrum and blur.
For his arm lifted up

by the latex-gloved hand, water poured past all thirst.
For the gloved hand,

the pale, powdery fingers of a terrible angel. For each
thumbprint bruise,

the petal of a dark rose. For his voice calling his mother,
the single note of a thrush.

For where they burned him, a choir of stars tangling
a high, unresolved chord.

For his round child's face, the low sough of an oboe.
For his eyes, a palm

to stroke them closed. A close-up to anoint orbital bone,
brow, mouth and chin;

Vaseline on the lens; a finger in ash to write his name.

Flame

for Fatima Omar Mahmud al-Najar, Palestinian martyr

Not the change but another
kind of pause: the body

in paraphrase, working loose
like a tooth,

hair releasing in drifts
like dead leaves

in late fall. They took it all,
leaving her

unable to eat even a mote,
burnt trunk and root.

But they forgot that what fire
eats it also ignites,

and so great a heat will anneal
sand and salt into glass

seamed and re-seamed
with healed fractures,

compressed into a dense lump
of quartz percussion-flaked

again and again to hone
the ritual blade,

human rage finally refined
into the clarity

of pure air, its precise blessing
folded and wrapped

about her slim waist, released
finally as black smoke

and silence, in one thin flame,
rising.

III

dolphin

deep in the cove   moves the curve
of a dolphin

her calf by her side   somewhere
in time you and I

moved like that   what matter that
you   my son   then

now   my daughter   on the beach
only the bony beak

& a few steps away the frail high
basket of rib-cage

that could belong to a human boy or girl
but for the fluke

valentine

petals of the pink camellia
plaster wet asphalt

each Magritte heart bent
off its vertical axis

sad valentines
posted to a wounded world

regret   the stone in my side
you my child leave

no thorn unturned   what
I know of dwarf stars

swallows your eyes when
you look into my face

then look away   is it fear
for me   or of me—

such dense collapsed darkness—
like crepe paper

and school paste these hearts
melt in the rain

free

begun when they cut her umbilicus
her separation from   me   but for years   we
were knitted up in (what i thought was)

love   he (who no longer is) said
the words like he meant them   a new child born
when s/he severed family

(specifically me)   at times like she's
gnawed off her own (or was it my) arm   to be free
& i don't know now what to do

with the photos & memories
of the child dressed always (I thought without ever
thinking) in little-boy-blue

but yes   also Brave-New-World
miraculous   like limb regeneration or Lady Lazarus
less reborn than restored

to the whole & intact if not before
seen or even   (forgive me)   imagined   you
my daughter   now

less & less the sleeping child
stolen from me   more & more   the child who
woke & was finally able to be

Echo

at the gorge in Truchas, New Mexico

The stone fit my hand. It had a hollow you could drink water
from or fill with sand.

I tucked it, fist-sized, inside my vest—baby borne in a sling,
damp weight on my chest—

the stone was cool and calm, and I felt something flow from me
into its hollow.

You: cells of my cells, blood of my blood, bone of my bone,
my flesh echo. The womb

is a semipermeable membrane, and an echo a voice that hears
what it calls. You made me

while I made you; nothing is owed. I came to the canyon rim
and saw how best to carry you: I let the stone go.

Prodigal

Everywhere all over mothers have wept
into their nightgown sleeves, hoping
not to wake those who slept beside them.
Cleave blood from blood, and you will bleed.
Let us believe again in waxen wings,
titanium-ribbed, that can fly near the sun
and never fail. In apostolic things—
Lazarus lifting her matted head
to call the blossoms in, loaves and fishes,
rain in seasons of drought, species of life
that do not wink out, one by one, like stars.
Medea's kids sung to and snug in their bed,
truth in the news, the world intact in a bead
of dew, and—bound fast again to me—you.

Failed Aubade

You in your blue-striped hospital blanket, face furled like a bud.
You in tiny sailor suit and cap,

in team jersey and sagging white pants, taking a mighty swing.
You, greaved in body armor

and sweat at lacrosse practice, suddenly taller than me. It is true
I rejoiced more in your gentleness

than in your beard, but still, I did rejoice in your beard, and also
in looking up at and leaning against you

in the way women are taught to look up to and lean against men.
Forgive me for that, daughter,

and for my grief at your loss even though you never left, even though
you always have been and are still here.

Moon

When I got the news you've decided you're no longer you,
not the you I gave birth to and watched grow from seed
to sapling to tree—that you never were *that* you—it was
as if my beloved had died. In the kingdom of childhood
there once lived a boy loved with my infinite heart.

Forfeit false memory. Forfeit eyes seeing absence in presence:
crepe on a mirror, black wreath on a door. Did I not hear
your voice just a moment ago? On the horizon
hangs a moon, tonight's fat fruit, tomorrow's pale rind.
Shall I mourn one, seeing the other?

You'll have curves soon, softer skin. Your voice will change
as it did once before and will still be your voice
as it was before. Your hands will still be your hands.
You come in, sit with me, eyes meeting mine
while you teach me the pronouns.

Outside, it wanes as it rises and swells as it sets, and yet,
the moon remains, and it remains the moon.

Sufferance

Transgender, as in counterfeit, as in someone *appearing*
or *attempting to be* a member

of the other gender, erroneously equated with *transsexual*
or cross-dresser or pervert or *predator.*

As in *a term used by ugly girls as a defense mechanism*
against prettier girls. As in

the solution lies in psychology or religion or, until 1960,
an icepick lobotomy

performed without anesthesia. As in *passive permission*
from lack of interference,

tolerance of something intolerable—the teen set on fire
at the back of the bus, the one stabbed

with a steak knife or scarred by acid—the way the world
daily scathes you, my fear for your safety

a daily sufferance, as in *endurance,* as in [archaic] *misery,*
as in Middle English or Latin equivalent

of *suffer,* akin in its way to *suffrage,* my right to vote.
As in vote for, support—daughter,

I want to support you in this—as in *ecclesiastical,* a prayer,
an *intercessory prayer or petition.*

Intercessory, come between. Intercede, yes—my body—
between yours—and—theirs.

Second Gratitude

I made soup tonight, with cabbage, chard
and thyme picked outside our back door.
For this moment the room is warm and light,
and I can presume you safe somewhere.
I know the night lives inside you. I know grave,
sad errors were made, dividing you, and hiding
you from you inside. I know a girl like you
was knifed last week, another set aflame.
I know I lack the words, or all the words I say
are wrong. I know I'll call and you won't answer,
and still I'll call. I want to tell you
you are loved with all I have, recklessly,
and with abandon, loved the way the cabbage
in my garden near-inverts itself, splayed
to catch each last ray of sun. And how
the feeling furling-in only makes the heart
more dense and green. Tonight it seems like
something one could bear.

Guess what, Dad and I finally figured out Pandora,
and after all those years of silence, our old music
fills the air. It fills the air, and somehow, here,
at this instant and for this instant only—
perhaps three bars—what I recall equals all I feel,
and I remember all the words.

Notes

"Only," page 1, owes a debt to Stanley Kunitz.

"The Unexploded Ordnance Bin," page 8. The Liberty Ship S.S. James Longstreet anchored off Wellfleet, Massachusetts, was used for target practice until 1970, and beachcombers still find ordnance often enough that the Police Station maintains a receptacle for its disposal and controlled detonation. Coastal areas of the United States harbor millions of pounds of dumped munitions dumped by the Military or fired during training missions.

"rapture / rupture," page 11, is after a line by Michelle Bitting from *Blue Laws* (Finishing Line Press 2007).

In "The Deer," page 13, the phrase "sigh of O" is from James Joyce's *Ulysses*.

"Compound. Depressed. Fracture," page 16 is for Elisabeth Murawski.

"Head Injury Odyssey," page 17, is for Joan Ryan and Barry Tompkins.

"Like Birders" page 18. Advocates on the autism spectrum believe that some things viewed as disabilities—for example, hyper focus and perseveration—are actually strengths, and that "normality" whitewashes a certain lack of passion and imagination in many neurotypicals.

"First Gratitude," page 19, is for Connie Post, fellow ASD mother-in-arms.

"Remembrance of Things Past," page 29, is dedicated to the Zamora family.

"Requiem Mass for the Yuma 14," page 30, is indebted to *The Devil's Highway: A True Story* (Little, Brown 2001) by Luis Alberto Urrea.

In "Sufferance," page 44, the italicized words are from definitions found in http://urbandictionary.com and http://dictionary.com.

Rebecca Foust's books include *The Unexploded Ordnance Bin,* winner of the 2018 Swan Scythe Press Chapbook Award and *Paradise Drive*, winner of the Press 53 Award for Poetry and reviewed in the *Times Literary Supplement.* Recognitions include the Cavafy and James Hearst Prizes (Poetry), the Lascaux and *American Literary Review* Prizes (Fiction), the Constance Rooke Creative Nonfiction Prize, and fellowships from The Frost Place, Hedgebrook, MacDowell, and Sewanee. New work is in *Alaska Quarterly Review, The Hudson Review, The Massachusetts Review, Southern Review, Zyzzyva,* and elsewhere. Foust was Marin County Poet Laureate in 2017-19 and works as Poetry Editor for *Women's Voices for Change* and as an assistant Editor for *Narrative Magazine.*

Lorna Stevens is a mixed media artist whose work has been acquired by the Brooklyn Museum, the di Rosa Center for Contemporary Art, the New York Public Library, the Numakunai Sculpture Garden, and SF MOMA's Research Library. She received her MFA from Columbia University and teaches at City College of San Francisco.